THEN & NOW®

PALM SPRINGS

OPPOSITE: Established in 1930, Smoke Tree Ranch became a "colony" for those who "have been every place, seen everything, and done most things." Industrialists, executives, President Eisenhower, and Walt Disney were attracted to the area by its unpretentious atmosphere and the chance to live a Western adventure. Walt and Lillian Disney purchased their first home in the colony in 1948 and, with their two daughters, enjoyed horseback riding, swimming, and communal meals. In this photograph, Walt is having a discussion with children of other "colonists" who went to school on the ranch. It is the Smoke Tree Ranch's "STR" brand that is emblazoned on the tie Walt wears while holding Mickey's hand in statues at Disney theme parks. (Palm Springs Historical Society, 10-016.)

PALM SPRINGS

Roger C. Palmer, PhD

For my partner, Rene Cua

Library of Congress Control Number: 2011932500

Published by Arcadia Publishing
Charleston, South Carolina

Printed in the United States of America

Then and Now is a registered trademark and is used under license from
Salamander Books Limited

For all general information, please contact Arcadia Publishing:
Telephone 843-853-2070
Fax 843-853-0044
E-mail sales@arcadiapublishing.com
For customer service and orders:
Toll-Free 1-888-313-2665

Visit us on the Internet at www.arcadiapublishing.com

ON THE FRONT COVER: The Mercado Plaza (141–185 South Palm Canyon Drive) is popular in downtown Palm Springs. It incorporates the mountain as a backdrop for its Mediterranean Eclectic–style architecture. Multiple restaurants feature Japanese cuisine, pizza, steaks as well as American fare with Coca-Cola posters of the 1940s. Trendy shops and specialty stores are designed with tourists in mind. The 1946 photograph of this location shows cottages at Nellie Coffman's Village Inn, a less expensive alternative to her Desert Inn one block north. (Palm Springs Historical Society, 59-108; 58-110.)

ON THE BACK COVER: Pueblo Revival, a favored style for Palm Canyon Drive architecture from the 1920s until the late 1940s, housed the Desert Camera Shop in this 1946 photograph. Bicycle riding, then and now, provides a convenient means of exercise and sightseeing. The nondescript building on the right was the Malt Shop, complete with teenagers and local police. Both buildings can be seen in their current form at 282–288 North Palm Canyon Drive. (Palm Springs Historical Society, 58-058c.)

CONTENTS

ACKNOWLEDGMENTS

The most important acknowledgement is to E. Stewart Williams and his family for their donation of the collection of Palm Canyon Drive images made in 1946 on which most of this book is based.

Jeri Vogelsang, the director of the Palm Springs Historical Society (PSHS), patiently answered many questions, suggested relevant materials, and proofed the manuscript. Thanks also go to Renee Brown, the PSHS assistant director, for giving suggestions; Nicolette Wenzell, everyone's go to for help, for providing access to her research regarding the Desert Inn, checking references willingly, and donating her proofing skills; Syd Smith, our volunteer expert in all things technical, for helping with scans of historical image; and Greg Hough, the president of the PSHS Board, as well as board member Jane Lykken Hoff, for reviewing text and images and providing suggestions.

The research for this book is based almost exclusively on newspaper clippings, files regarding local architects, and local family history files maintained by the PSHS. Collections of early telephone directories and city directories were constant resources for confirmations of addresses, names, and dates. Articles and advertisements in the collection of Palm Springs *Villager* magazines were helpful in documenting postwar life in Palm Springs. Also useful were the local history vertical files donated by the Palm Springs Public Library to PSHS. Of great help were the "Prickly Pears" interviews, conducted in the mid-1980s by the Palm Springs Public Library, with more than 50 citizens who contributed their personal experiences of life in Palm Springs and the people and events that shaped its history (now available on DVD at the library). Very useful was a publication entitled *Class One*, which was about historical buildings and was published by the Palm Springs Preservation Foundation; its paperbacks about local architects, such as E. Stewart Williams, were also beneficial. Also helpful were Palm Springs episodes of Huell Howser's public television program, *Palm Springs Week.* Thanks go to Patrick McGrew for explaining the footprint of "the Center" and the buildings included in a preservation initiative. The book *Palm Springs Weekend* by Alan Hess and Andrew Danish was helpful for putting a context around the development of Modernist architecture in Palm Springs. Of significant benefit was access to PSHS Collections Management System for instant access to the growing collections of cataloged items.

All photographs are from the collections of the Palm Springs Historical Society, all rights reserved. In parentheses, following each caption, is/are the digital archive record number(s) for referenced photographs, e.g. (58-045; 59-045.). The author's portion of the royalties for this book is assigned to the Palm Springs Historical Society.

—Roger C. Palmer, PhD
Volunteer Registrar and Member of the Board
Palm Springs Historical Society

INTRODUCTION

For the opening of the 2009–2010 season of the Palm Springs Historical Society Museums, a new exhibit, *Palm Canyon Drive: Then and Now*, was mounted. Donated by architect E. Stewart Williams and his family, more than 140 negatives and photographs, taken in 1946 to document the buildings for the five core commercial blocks of downtown Palm Springs, form the basis for the exhibit. The 160 images in this book were selected from the photographs included in this popular display and represent the more than 60 years since the original images were made. Six additional historical photographs introduce the book and each of the five chapters. The arrangement within each chapter of this book shows the west side of Palm Canyon Drive on even pages and the east side of the street on odd-numbered pages. The "then" photographs are in sepia and generally are larger than the "now" photographs. Thus, the book is arranged to provide a historical and visual self-guided "walking tour" at a particular point in time (1946) counterpointed with the present. The book, in text and pictures, attempts to present a straightforward account of the core business district of Palm Springs as it emerged from World War II and the same five blocks today.

Palm Springs, California, is derived from the lands of the Agua Caliente band of Cahuilla Indians. For hundreds of years, the Agua Caliente lived in isolation from other cultures and enjoyed peaceful relations within the larger complex of Cahuilla Indian bands. In 1876, the US government deeded portions of Cahuilla land to the tribe as a "homeland" and also gave the Southern Pacific Railroad sections to encourage settlement of the West. A "checkerboard" arrangement for organizing the land provided the railroad with odd-numbered sections; even-numbered sections were given to the Indians. The Agua Caliente band of Cahuilla Indians became a "ward" of the federal government with their lands held in trust by the Bureau of Indian Affairs.

In 1885, John Guthrie McCallum bought Section 15 and other landholdings from the Southern Pacific Railroad. It was the purchase of this land by McCallum that established the foundation for a growing presence of settlers in the area. McCallum convinced Welwood Murray to build the first Palm Springs Hotel on land he sold to Murray. Today, the historic business district of Palm Springs is on Section 15 (Alejo Road to Ramon Road and Indian Avenue to the mountain).

At the turn of the 20th century, artists, such as prolific painter Carl Eytel, arrived to record the beauty of his newly discovered desert surroundings, while cartoonist Jimmy Swinnerton captured the foibles of fellow desert denizens. Chroniclers, such as J. Smeaton Chase, wrote of and photographed their desert travels. Some came seeking relief from chronic respiratory problems at Dr. Harry and Nellie Coffman's hotel and sanatorium (later to become the Desert Inn). Soon, the movie industry appeared with actors and staff to work on location and enjoy resorts constructed for their amusement. Photographers, such as Fred Clatworthy (*National Geographic*) and Stephen H. Willard, flourished. Others joined together to forge a close-knit and separate community of shared values and live-in stone houses without amenities. Main Street became Palm Canyon Drive in 1930. Rich industrialists from the East, Midwest, and West came to experience ranch life, horses, rodeos, and outdoor cookouts. The village became the city of Palm Springs in 1938. Veterans returning from World War II significantly expanded the population and created the need for more housing and services. Architects, such as E. Stewart Williams, Bill Cody, John Porter Clark, Albert Frey, Richard Harrison, Robson Chambers, and Roger Williams, experimented with Modernist architecture and employed Palm Springs as a stage upon which to construct mid-century Desert Modern homes and commercial and public buildings.

For the five blocks that are both the core of downtown Palm Springs and the focus of this book, there are several recurring names. In addition to McCallum and Murray, McCallum's daughter Pearl, with her husband, Austin McManus, developed her father's landholdings from the 1920s to the 1960s. Nellie Coffman, with clear and persistent vision, created the Desert Inn. From tent house beginnings in 1909, a world-class resort emerged by the time of her death in 1950. The White sisters brought wealth and a desire to improve their surroundings and the lives of neighbors. Dr. Florilla White, first of the sisters to visit, stayed at Murray's hotel in 1912. She returned to the village in 1913 with her sister Cornelia, who was recovering after escaping an American colony in Mexico threatened by the Mexican Revolution. In 1917, the last sister to arrive was Isabel, the only one to marry. She and J. Smeaton Chase had but five years before his passing but they are remembered to have been very happy. Cornelia helped make possible the Welwood Murray Memorial Library and the original Palm Springs Desert Museum. It was on her land that the La Plaza shopping center was built in 1936. Zaddie Bunker arrived in the village in 1913 with self-confidence and ample common sense. She turned a rented alfalfa field into a local real estate empire. The deaths of Cornelia White in 1961, Pearl McManus in 1966, and Zaddie Bunker in 1969 marked the end of an era.

Change in Palm Springs has been a way of life since Murray built the first hotel. In recent decades, thousands have arrived to provide the services needed by an expanding population of seasonal "snowbirds" escaping winter winds and an ever-increasing rush of tourists, permanent residents, and retirees. Around 20,000 tourists visited in 1922. Today, approximately one million tourists stay in Palm Springs hotels annually, and 600,000 stay in non-hotel accommodations. There is an expanding gay presence in all aspects of the political and cultural life of Palm Springs. Gays serve on the Palm Springs City Council, and the last two mayors were openly gay; many are active in preserving Palm Springs' history and architectural heritage. At the same time, the Agua Caliente band of Cahuilla Indians exercise control over the commercial and residential development of their lands. They own major areas of Palm Springs, including Section 14 (Alejo Road to Ramon Road and Indian Avenue to Sunrise Way) adjacent to the historic Section 15 business district. With leasing revenues from the landholdings, two casinos, and other business interests, they are one of the largest employers in the area and a driving force behind a variety of cultural activities.

The 1946 photographs in this book reveal village-sized, family-owned, locally run businesses; five service stations; two newspapers; doctors' offices; chiropractor's office; movie theaters; upscale hotels; small hotels; tourist courts; apartment complex; night club; cafés; delicatessen; malt shop; small department stores; numerous specialty shops; beauty shops; a building housing a music shop, bowling alley, and a barbershop; radio shop; camera shop; waffle shop; news store; and real estate offices. One bank provided financial services. One building housed the fire and police departments. The chamber of commerce had a building of its own. All of this in five downtown blocks. America won World War II, and everything changed.

CHAPTER 1

100 SOUTH PALM CANYON DRIVE

John Guthrie McCallum brought his wife, Emily, three sons, and two daughters to land acquired in 1884 from the Southern Pacific Railroad. Their adobe, the oldest building in Palm Springs, was moved and rebuilt on the Village Green (221 South Palm Canyon Drive). This Class One Historic Site serves as a museum and headquarters of the Palm Springs Historical Society. (15-004.)

Tahquitz Canyon Way, looking west, divides 101 South (left) from 101 North Palm Canyon Drive. After 1909, much of the block to the north became Nellie Coffman's Desert Inn. After McCallum failed in his Palm Springs ventures, his daughter Pearl McCallum McManus (1879–1966) and her husband, Austin McManus, developed her father's landholdings on the block to the south and elsewhere in Palm Springs. By 1925, the Oasis Hotel extended from 101 to 139 South Palm Canyon Drive. (59-099; 58-099.)

Tahquitz Canyon Way, looking east, divides 100 North (left) from 100 South Palm Canyon Drive. On the land acquired by Welwood Murray from John McCallum, Murray built his Victorian-style Palm Springs Hotel. Sisters Dr. Florilla White and Cornelia White bought the 100 North Palm Canyon Drive block in 1914 from Murray for $10,000. The block to the south was undeveloped, but Cornelia purchased most of it from the Murray estate for $5,000. (58-045; 59-045.)

Pearl and Austin McManus met with Frank Lloyd Wright's son Lloyd in 1922. The Lloyd Wright–designed Oasis Hotel opened in 1925 at 101–139 South Palm Canyon Drive (called Main Street until 1930). The Oasis Hotel has been called, "One of the greatest Modern designs of the 1920s in California." By 1952, the owner of the Oasis, the Western Hotel Corporation, had decided to replace a portion of the hotel with the Oasis Office Building, designed by architects Williams, Williams & Williams. (58-100; 59-100.)

In 1938, George Murray, son of Welwood, gave the city land he owned at 100 South Palm Canyon Drive for the construction of a library. Modernist architect Albert Frey submitted sketches, but library board member Nellie Coffman ruled in favor of a building resembling a little house. John Porter Clark, city resident architect, designed the resulting Welwood Murray Memorial Library, a Class One Historic Site. Built at a cost of $25,000, it opened in early 1941. (59-115a; 58-115a.)

The portion of the original Oasis Hotel at 121 South Palm Canyon Drive is a Class One Historic Site. The tower, still covered with foliage camouflage to protect against air attack in the 1946 photograph, can be seen clearly in the contemporary image. The structure was built using a slip-form method of construction. A 12-inch layer of wall was poured into form boards, and when the concrete was dry, the boards were slipped up to form another tier. (59-103; 58-103.)

The 1946 photograph shows a building at 116 South Palm Canyon Drive that once housed the studio of local photographer Stephen Willard. In 1989, Wessman Development designed La Plaza de las Flores for this location. Next door is the first of several buildings in the La Plaza project; it opened in 1936 at 124 South Palm Canyon Drive and is sometimes referred to as the first self-contained shopping center in Southern California. (58-116; 59-116.)

The Modernist design of the Oasis Hotel highlights a rivalry between Pearl McManus and Nellie Coffman, who had selected Mission Revival for her buildings at the Desert Inn one block north. In these photographs of 125–139 South Palm Canyon Drive, there are four rooms that were part of the Oasis Hotel. They were transformed for commercial use many years ago. In the contemporary photograph, the front wall of the building affords a view of the original tiered concrete construction. (58-104; 59-104.)

Julia Carnell, a major stockholder in National Cash Register and frequent winter visitor to the Desert Inn, facilitated construction of La Plaza. She chose a Spanish Eclectic style and Dayton, Ohio, architect Harry Williams to plan La Plaza. The Plaza Theatre at 128 South Palm Canyon Drive opened in 1936. That venue was restored in 1990 for the first Palm Springs International Film Festival and, in 1992, this Class One Historic Site became home to the Fabulous Palm Springs Follies. (59-116x; 58-116x.)

Nellie Coffman operated the Village Inn from the 1920s to mid-1940s where she offered a lower-cost alternative to her Desert Inn. The Village Inn cottages were relocated from the Desert Inn to the Village Inn as part of a major 1920s upscale redesign of the Desert Inn. From 1947 until 1993, Bullock's department store occupied 300 feet of former Village Inn frontage. Since 1998, the Mercado Plaza has occupied this location at 155 South Palm Canyon Drive. (59-105; 58-105.)

Harry Williams and architect son Roger flew to Santa Barbara to study examples of Spanish design. Engineers researched the effects of earthquakes on buildings in Long Beach where a quake had struck two years earlier. Knowledge gained was incorporated into the final design of La Plaza. There are few changes between the 1946 photograph and the present beyond new plate-glass windows and doors to provide better access for sidewalk cafés and shops at 132–142 South Palm Canyon Drive. (58-117; 59-117.)

The Mercado Plaza was designed and developed by Altevers Associates Architects for Wessman Development Company. Mayor William Kleindienst (1995–2003) spearheaded support for downtown revitalization efforts, including the Mercado Plaza project, which follows a Mediterranean Eclectic style in a group of buildings on the former sites of the Village Inn (until 1947) and Bullock's department store (demolition permit issued in 1993) at 155 South Palm Canyon Drive. (58-106; 59-106.)

La Plaza was designed to attract wealthy visitors from coastal cities in Southern California. Second-floor penthouses and ground-floor cottages provided accommodations for the well to do, and a dormitory facility was for their chauffeurs. The 1946 photograph shows the studio of Bernard of Hollywood, renowned photographer of movie stars. Next door is the office of Robert Ransom, the leading realtor in Palm Springs during the 1930s. The spaces are now occupied by a popular shop for sandals and a café. (59-118; 58-118.)

Foliage flourished on the grounds of the many small hotels that once dotted Palm Canyon Drive. The desert fan palm, *Washingtonia filifera*, is native to Palm Springs and its canyons. Over the decades, creosote bushes, palo verde trees, date palms, oleanders, and Mexican pepper trees, among others, were much in evidence. It was in 1949 that the first major project to plant and maintain palm trees was funded by the city and launched along Palm Canyon Drive. (59-107; 58-107.)

La Plaza, as a self-contained shopping center, provided underground parking, a gas station, restaurant, dance hall, shops, post office, and a shoe-shine stand. Little architectural change has occurred at 144 South Palm Canyon Drive in the transformation of the Yarn Shop to See's Candy. In 1939, Frank Bogert became the first manager of the Palm Springs Chamber of Commerce. The penthouse above the Yarn Shop was provided free of charge to Bogert as part of his compensation. (58-119; 59-119.)

Village Inn cottages were moved to East Ramon Road in 1947 to provide housing for Desert Inn staff and space for a new department store. Los Angeles architects Wurdeman and Becket designed Bullock's in the late Moderne style. From 1947 until the early 1990s, Bullock's occupied 141 to 185 South Palm Canyon Drive, ultimately failing in its motto "to build a business which shall know no end." It was replaced in 1998 with the Mercado Plaza. (46-079; 59-108.)

La Plaza is a Class One Historic Site. Aboveground parking at La Plaza remains as designed in 1936. Then and now, the road to the left extends from Indian Canyon Drive to Palm Canyon Drive. The road to the right is one way in the opposite direction. At street level, the buildings on either side variously have accommodated the Palm Springs Post Office, a grocery store, insurance offices, and shops. (59-121; 58-121.)

The building housing the Bullock's department store did not survive the changing priorities of its owners as they juggled the futures of several department store brands under their corporate umbrellas. The owners of Mercado Plaza have the advantage of many tenants with diverse businesses; they are not dependent on a single corporate entity to sustain their viability and can, as they have, attract new tenants when others depart. (59-109; 58-109.)

From its opening in 1936 until 2005, Desmond's department store was a tenant of La Plaza. It was popular for its upscale American-made clothing brands and resort wear. At 12,000 square feet, it had the largest footprint of any of the La Plaza retailers. The vacancy created by its passing has not reduced the popularity of the shopping center. Preparations are underway to subdivide the space for new shops. (58-123; 59-123.)

From late fall until early spring, when the Follies stage show is playing, buses arrive in Palm Springs with tourists looking for nostalgia. Those who have tickets for the show have lunch at one of the several restaurants at La Plaza or across the street at Mercado Plaza. Shops on both sides of the block cater to tourists looking for colorful hats, dresses, sandals, and cowboy attire. (58-110; 59-110.)

Except for larger display windows and a new font for its name, little changed in the former Desmond's facade over the 70 years it served generations of shoppers. A small water fountain for dogs was built into the left base of the Desmond's building. It was excavated recently but is no longer operational. La Plaza extends along South Palm Canyon Drive to 184 South Palm Canyon Drive. (59-125; 58-125.)

In 1956, the Palm Springs *Villager* magazine published, "Palm Canyon Drive—The World's Most Beautiful Shopping Street." Four of the five photographs included in the article show streetscapes of the 100 block of South Palm Canyon Drive (two photographs of the La Plaza shopping center [1936], Bullock's [1947], and the ground-floor retail space of the Oasis Office Building [1952]). At that time, Palm Springs was experiencing a Modernism design and construction boom for commercial buildings, civic spaces, and homes. (59-111; 58-111.)

A building was constructed from 186 to 198 South Palm Canyon Drive at about the same time as the construction of La Plaza but was not part of that project. Sam Maloof purchased the entire building in 1943. With his wife, Sophia, and children, Gerry and Joyce, he operated a department store at 186–190. By 1973, Gerry assumed management of the store, which was downsized to specialize in men's wear. Tony's Men's Wear now is located here. (58-126; 59-126.)

187–189 South Palm Canyon Drive was the address in the Palm Springs' city directory in 1941 for residential real estate owned by Lila O'Kelly. Leo Baker and Sam Stewart acquired the property, demolished the house, and built a retail gift and liquor store called the Cantina. The single Modernist building now at this location is believed to have dated from 1949 or 1950. (58-112; 59-112.)

With the incorporation of the city of Palm Springs in 1938, the dividing line between north and south moved two blocks south from Amado Road to Tahquitz Canyon Way. The city directory for 1937 lists Valentine's Pharmacy at 360 South Palm Canyon Drive, but in the subsequent directory, the address became 198 South Palm Canyon Drive. The name changed to Tahquitz Pharmacy by 1940. External modifications for 186 to 198 South Palm Canyon Drive included modernized windows and the addition of a tile-covered walkway. (59-129; 58-129.)

Prior to 1950, residential housing was located at 191–193 South Palm Canyon Drive. In 1950, the city directory listed a vacancy at 191 and the Royal Palm Galleries at 193. A magazine article published shortly after its construction designated Modernist architect William F. Cody as the building's designer. Until recently, an art gallery occupied the entire ground floor. New owners are refurbishing the building and restoring lost detail. (59-114; 58-114.)

CHAPTER 2

100 NORTH PALM CANYON DRIVE

Nellie Coffman (1867–1950) arrived with vision, energy, and integrity. She founded a boardinghouse and sanatorium in 1909 comprised of tent houses purchased in Los Angeles for $85 each. As the number, wealth, and health of guests grew ("no invalids"), cottages replaced tents. By 1928, newly constructed Mission Revival buildings housed Desert Inn guests in rooms, suites, and apartments. (07-267.)

During World War II, the American Red Cross was located at 107 North Palm Canyon Drive. The Desert Inn owned the property immediately adjacent to its front gates but occupied 33 acres behind other properties facing Palm Canyon Drive. When Nellie Coffman died in 1950, Desert Inn management was assumed by her sons George Roberson (1888–1968) and Owen Earl Coffman (1892–1967). In the contemporary photograph, a bank, built in 1968, has sat vacant since 1992, awaiting a new direction. (58-002; 59-002.)

Behind the fence in this 1946 photograph is the original Welwood Murray Palm Springs Hotel, which opened for business by 1893. The hotel was purchased in 1914 by sisters Dr. Florilla and Cornelia White. Under their ownership, except for select land fronting Palm Canyon Drive, most of the property was not developed for commercial use. Low-rise commercial buildings are now located where the hotel once stood. (59-046; 58-046.)

Victory having been achieved, the American Legion Lounge for military men and women at 111 North Palm Canyon Drive awaited a new use in 1946. Four years later, Nellie Coffman died leaving her sons to carry on the business. In 1955, the Desert Inn was sold to actress Marion Davies, who began to transform the property into a New York–themed fantasy. In the contemporary photograph, vacant space for a restaurant occupies the site of the former American Legion. (59-003; 58-003.)

At the age of seven, Paul Grimm arrived in the United States from South Africa. He trained as an artist and spent several years painting backdrops for movie studios in Los Angeles. He moved to Palm Springs in 1932 and is noted especially for his Southern California desert paintings. He lived here until his death in 1974. His studio was located at 122 North Palm Canyon Drive in 1946. Currently, low-rise retail shops occupy this location. (58-048; 59-048.)

In 1946, the Willows gift shop was located at 137 North Palm Canyon Drive. By 1960, the illness of Marion Davies brought about the sale of the Desert Inn to George Alexander, a builder of Modernist home developments in the 1950s. A $10-million plan for a Desert Inn Fashion Plaza was developed to include retail shops, a convention center, hotel, and parking. The contemporary photograph shows a low-rise building housing retail space and a popular pizza restaurant. (58-004; 59-004.)

The H.H. Fowler real estate office occupied 130 North Palm Canyon Drive in 1946. The vegetation on the other side of the fence is part of the original Palm Springs Hotel. In 1938, Cornelia White offered the land on this site for use as a park if the city would pay the taxes. The offer was rejected as the city coped with limited revenues. The small shops now along Palm Canyon Drive remain popular with visiting tourists. (59-049; 58-049.)

In 1946, Thompson's Fine Candies occupied a shop at 145 North Palm Canyon Drive. By 1965, following the untimely death of developer George Alexander, Home Savings and Loan acquired the Desert Inn property for $3.5 million. Plans were prepared by developer Joseph K. Eichenbaum and architect Charles Luckman for the Desert Inn Fashion Plaza. Demolition of the Desert Inn began in 1966. One- and two-story commercial spaces now occupy this location. (59-005; 58-005.)

A strong desire for sweets can be surmised from this 1946 photograph of Fun in the Sun Candies at 132 North Palm Canyon Drive. The Desert Sweet Shop was just a few doors up the street, and Thompson's Candy Shop was across the street. Waffles, a "Do-Nut" shop, and Riviera Ice Cream were not far away. Low-rise shops now occupy this location. (58-009; 59-009.)

The main gate of the Desert Inn was located at 153 North Palm Canyon Drive. The Mission Revival upgrade that had been made in the 1920s finally was repaid in 1946 with money Nellie Coffman received from the sale of the Village Inn property on South Palm Canyon Drive. By 1968, various enterprises began opening in the $25-million Desert Inn Fashion Plaza. A 2009 photograph shows an office where the Desert Inn gates once stood. (07-200; 59-006a.)

The Cottage Delicatessen was located at 138 North Palm Canyon Drive when this photograph was taken in early 1946. In the city directory for 1941–1942, this location is listed as R.B. Cregar Indian Art Goods and in the 1946–1947 directory as Mary Helen's Children's Shop. The deli was at this location during World War II years and served civilian government workers and military service men and women. Low-rise retail space can be seen in the contemporary photograph. (59-051; 58-051.)

Philip Boyd arrived at the Desert Inn with respiratory problems in 1921. After having worked with the chamber of commerce with the help of Nellie Coffman, he eventually resolved the unwillingness of banks to open a Palm Springs office. Nellie introduced Boyd to Mario Gianini, son of the Bank of America founder. A local office was opened, and within a year, a total of $1 million was in local accounts. Boyd was manager from 1929 to 1934. Low-rise retail space can be seen in the contemporary photograph. (59-006b; 58-006b.)

In 1934, Kenneth Colborn announced the "Palm Springs Shops Building" designed by C. Allan Tierney (144–160 North Palm Canyon Drive), as seen in the 1946 photograph. The contemporary photograph shows a building that opened in 1950 as the new branch of Bank of America (146–150 North Palm Canyon Drive). The architects for this International-style design were Archibald Quincy Jones (1913–1979) and Paul Revere Williams (1894–1980), the first African American to become a member and fellow of the American Institute of Architects. (58-052; 59-052.)

Until January 1948, when Bullock's opened a new store on South Palm Canyon Drive, they maintained a small department store on the grounds of the Desert Inn at 163 North Palm Canyon Drive. By 1978, Home Savings and Loan sold the Desert Inn Fashion Plaza for $7 million to a Los Angeles partnership. The contemporary photograph shows continuation of retail and office space along the western side of North Palm Canyon Drive. (58-007; 59-007.)

When Jones and Williams began work on the Center (156–174 North Palm Canyon Drive and 167–181 North Indian Canyon), the first of the twin buildings (156–166 North Palm Canyon Drive), as seen in the contemporary photograph, incorporated elements from Colborn's Palm Springs Shops Building. The Center is sometimes referred to as the Town & Country Center after a restaurant with that name located in the rear courtyard. (59-052a; 58-052a.)

In 1946, the upscale Desert Inn Beauty Salon occupied 173 North Palm Canyon Drive. By 1980, the Los Angeles partnership that owned the Desert Inn Fashion Plaza also had acquired the Palm Springs Hotel at 257 North Palm Canyon Drive. That was seen as a first step in the potential acquisition of the entire 201 block. In the contemporary photograph, retail and office space continue. (59-008; 58-008.)

When construction began in 1948 on the Center, the Bank of America branch serving Palm Springs was demolished. In the contemporary photograph, the 20-foot-wide passageway leading to the rear courtyard can be seen. By 2007, Wessman Development had previously acquired the site for redevelopment. Preservationists seek to prevent loss of the Center by having it classified as a historic site. The issue remains unresolved. (58-053; 59-053.)

The Village Coffee Shop at 181 North Palm Canyon Drive was built on land acquired in 1929 by the Desert Inn. It was a popular meeting place for lunch during and after World War II. In 1980, as part of efforts for an expanded Desert Inn Fashion Plaza, the local redevelopment agency was authorized to help developers acquire the additional property needed for a potential project. In the contemporary photograph, retail and office space continue. (58-009; 59-009.)

Carl Lykken built Lykken's dry goods store on land acquired from Cornelia White in 1914; a hardware section was added in 1917. Until the late 1920s, he had the only telephone in town. A 1930s redesign added arches, but the building has not been altered since; original clay roof tiles are still in place. This Class One Historic Site is located at 180 North Palm Canyon Drive. In the contemporary photograph, a toy store occupies the location. (59-054; 58-054.)

The Desert Inn Garage at 193 North Palm Canyon Drive sold gasoline, provided automobile services, and was the home of a Buick dealership in the 1946 photograph. By the early 1980s, a major chain expressed interest in relocating to a new shopping plaza downtown, which was then under consideration by the city and owners of the Desert Inn Fashion Plaza. The contemporary photograph shows the 50,000-square-foot vacant store now at this location. (59-010; 58-010.)

In 1934, Desert Inn winter guest Julia Carnell of Dayton, Ohio, launched her first project in Palm Springs with architect Harry Williams. She paid $40,000 for the former Community Church, and Williams designed the Carnell Building (188–196 North Palm Canyon Drive) with multiple shops. The second floor was fitted with 13 offices and 5 apartments. Every room was provided with the latest light fixtures, electric heating, and air conditioning. Examination of the two photographs reveals only cosmetic exterior changes. (58-055; 59-055.)

In 1946, Andreas Road separated the Desert Inn Garage from the Village Pharmacy at 201 North Palm Canyon Drive. By the early 1980s, merchants in the 201 block objected to the closure of Andreas Road and proposed expansion of the Desert Inn Fashion Plaza. City officials contended that "redevelopment is needed downtown for the area to keep pace with planned commercial developments in Palm Desert and other tourist areas." The contemporary photograph shows continuation of retail and office space. (58-011; 59-011.)

200 NORTH PALM CANYON DRIVE

Zaddie Bunker (1887–1969) arrived in 1913 with a husband, Chauncey, daughter Frances, and self-study mechanical repair expertise. By 1929, Bunker's Garage housed the Bank of America local office. In 1932, Zaddie received a $30,000 loan to build the Village Theatre. In 1933, a Valerie Jean Date Shop replaced the bank, and the theater opened under manager Earle Strebe, the son-in-law of Zaddie. (28-114.)

Across the street, the Village Pharmacy occupied 201 North Palm Canyon Drive when this 1948 photograph was taken. In 1983, the Los Angeles partnership that owned the Desert Inn Fashion Plaza partnered with a large Ohio corporation to demolish the Desert Inn Fashion Plaza and replace buildings from 111 to 299 North Palm Canyon Drive with an enclosed mall, six-story hotel, and underground parking. In the contemporary photograph, retail space continues. (59-012a; 02-123.)

Looking east, Andreas Road was a two-way street, and there was still a military presence in Palm Springs, as seen in the 1946 photograph. The foot traffic and large number of parked cars indicate significant activity downtown. The view in the contemporary photograph reveals a one-way street enhanced with palm trees, benches, and attractive streetlights. The Carnell Building can be seen on the right in both photographs. (58-056; 59-056.)

Built on land owned by Zaddie Bunker, the Chi Chi was established in the mid-1930s and grew prosperous as a bar, restaurant, and world-class nightclub at 217 North Palm Canyon Drive. It was famous for entertainers, such as Jack Benny, when this 1946 photograph was taken.

By 1985, the Desert Fashion Plaza absorbed the 101 to 299 blocks and dropped "Inn" from its name. In the contemporary photograph, Desert Fashion Plaza retail and office space continue. (58-012b; 59-012b.)

The Royal Palms Hotel had rooms above the ground-floor shops at 218–226 North Palm Canyon Drive, as seen in this 1946 photograph. A second-floor sun deck shaded the sidewalk below. Villagers spoke of sports and the weather in front of the news shop. Some cooled themselves with soft drinks from the Orange Julius. The contemporary photograph reveals the elimination of hotel rooms and the sun deck. Homely shops for locals are now trendy outlets for tourists. (59-058a; 58-058a.)

An open window at the El Rey Hotel (245 North Palm Canyon Drive) and a c. 1940 Packard 120 are highlights of this 1946 photograph. According to a 1984 press release, the Desert Fashion Plaza was planned to expand from 140,000 to 295,000 square feet and increase retailers from 60 to 110. Originally developed as part of the Desert Fashion Plaza, the contemporary photograph shows the attractively updated Hyatt Regency Suites, which opened in 1985 as Maxim's. (59-016; 58-016.)

In 1946, Indianoya was one of several "Indian trading posts" in Palm Springs emphasizing Western themes. The "posts" were aimed at tourists and often were housed in Pueblo Revival–style buildings, as is the case here. Note that in the contemporary photograph, the bones of the building remain, but paint and trim have made a major thematic shift to appeal to an entirely different demographic. The building is located at 234 North Palm Canyon Drive. (58-058c; 59-058c.)

Shirlee's Beauty Salon and Brock's Waffle Shop were typical of the locally owned small businesses that propelled the economy of 1946 Palm Springs. By the mid-1990s, owners of the Desert Fashion Plaza sought to legalize slot machines for use in the property. After the measure failed, the mall was put on the market and sold for $14 million to a San Diego corporation in 1998. The contemporary photograph shows a continuation of the Hyatt Regency Suites. (58-020; 59-020)

Originally built as Palm Springs Harry's Café in 1927, it was here that Harry Mutascio served Italian and American food to Bette Davis, Tom Mix, and Gen. George S. Patton (who was in the desert training troops during World War II). The 1946 photograph was taken after Irwin Rubenstein transformed the restaurant into Ruby's Dunes. The contemporary photograph shows an English pub now occupying 238 North Palm Canyon Drive. (59-059; 58-059.)

There were several service stations in the center of Palm Springs in 1946; shown here is the Standard Station at 295 North Palm Canyon Drive. By 2001, the Desert Fashion Plaza, nearly empty for two years, was sold to Wessman Development. In 2007, John Wessman announced a $500-million to $700-million project to replace the Desert Fashion Plaza with integrated design approaches, including residential, commercial, and cultural facilities, within an ample open space environment. (59-022; 58-022.)

The 1946 photograph, also featured on the back cover, shows a Pueblo Revival–style building. It housed the Desert Camera Shop, which regularly advertised 24-hour film developing in the Palm Springs *Villager* magazine. The contemporary photograph shows a renovation that added a room but subtracted style. All three buildings in the photograph, including the cottage in the rear and the boxy building, which once housed the Malt Shop, are located at 282–288 North Palm Canyon Drive. (58-067b; 59-067b.)

Only the mountain remains unchanged in this view of Amado Road looking west. In 1946, Standard Service was on the left at 295 North Palm Canyon Drive, and Union was on the right at 301. With the economic turmoil of 2008 and beyond, Desert Fashion Plaza revitalization plans were shelved. Discussions are underway among Wessman Development, city officials, planning groups, preservationist interests, and others to reformulate planning initiatives, but uncertainty persists on many levels. (58-023; 59-023.)

CHAPTER

4

300 NORTH PALM CANYON DRIVE

The Palm Springs Chamber of Commerce, started in 1918, was located at 363 North Palm Canyon Drive in 1946. Next door was the telephone company building, and just north of that were the fire and police departments. Prior to incorporation in 1938, the chamber of commerce, with many volunteers and several committees, managed village services rather than village promotion. (28-245.)

In 1946, a Union service station was located at 301 North Palm Canyon Drive. The photograph shows why there has been a persistent desire among many to keep the beauty of the mountain exposed. The contemporary photograph shows the unique architecture of a building constructed in 1999. Commercial expansion in Section 15, the core commercial business district, increasingly has taken into consideration the mountain and surrounding Indian-owned lands. (59-024; 58-024.)

The 1946 photograph shows the Associated Service Station, which opened in 1934 under the ownership of Earl Hough at 300 North Palm Canyon Drive. Low-rise shops now dominate this block. In 1938, the city recorded a value of $375,000 for building permits. This fell to $58,533 in 1943 with the country at war. However, federal construction, exempt from local reporting, added many wartime facilities to Palm Springs. In 1946, with the war over, building permits rose to $6,680,000. (58-071; 59-071.)

In 1946, the Waikiki Restaurant was one of many Pacific-themed restaurants and resort wear shops that prospered in Palm Springs over the years. The contemporary photograph shows the unique architecture of Amado Plaza, which blends with many and varied views of the mountains. There was a dramatic rise in assessed valuations for Palm Springs from prewar to postwar years. Between 1939 and 1946, assessed valuations for Palm Springs rose from $6,740,870 to $13,564,040. (58-025a; 59-025a.)

The El Morocco Hotel at 336 North Palm Canyon Drive featured a recessed entrance and second-floor sun decks. Over the years between 1946 and the present, the contemporary photograph shows a building that has eliminated the hotel. Significant events in the chronology of Palm Springs include the arrival of electricity (1923), natural gas (1929), California Water and Telephone Company (1930), Western Airline Service (1945), and the first city manager (1946). (59-077; 58-077.)

The 1946 photograph shows a Mercury coupe parked in front of the Sunshine Court at 343 North Palm Canyon Drive. As the contemporary photograph illustrates, Amado Plaza (333 North Palm Canyon Drive) extends in multiple segments along the block. Developers desired Indian land for projects, but it was not realistic until President Eisenhower signed the Indian Leasing Act in 1959. Possibilities for commercial development on Indian land became economically feasible with a new maximum 99-year term. (59-027; 58-027.)

This Class One Historic Site at 342 North Palm Canyon Drive is the last example of Art Deco commercial architecture in downtown Palm Springs. The architect and builder are unknown. The first known owner was Clarence Simpson, who ran Simpson's Radio and Frigidaire until his death in 1944. Ted Reed then took over and operated from the location until he moved across the street in 1950. The Cork 'n Bottle moved into this building in 1950. (58-078; 59-078.)

The *Desert Sun* has been in many Palm Springs locations over its long history. It was started in 1927 and sold at the time this photograph was taken in 1946. The Streamline Moderne building, seen here, was located at 359 North Palm Canyon Drive, a few steps from the chamber of commerce, telephone company, fire department, and police department. Amado Plaza, now at this location, was constructed in 1979. (58-029; 59-029.)

From 1942 to 1945, Palm Springs was on active duty. The Railway Express Agency at 354 North Palm Canyon Drive was built during World War II. An airport was built for the Army Air Corps' 21st Ferrying Group, which included many pilots from the Women Air Service Pilots (WASP). The El Mirador Hotel became Torney General Hospital for war casualties. A waste treatment plant was added for the hospital and was turned over to the city following the end of the war. (59-080; 58-080.)

This Class One Historic Site at 365 North Palm Canyon Drive was constructed in 1934 to house California Water and Telephone Company. The Spanish Eclectic building is made of poured-in-place concrete. Later, California Water and Telephone Company became part of General Telephone, eventually emerging as GTE; however, the current provider is Verizon. While the building's exterior remains faithful to its original design, the interior was extensively redesigned to become the popular Azul and Alibi restaurant and bar. (59-031; 58-031.)

The Sportsman's Rifle Range and Canyon Café were located at 366 and 370 North Palm Canyon Drive when this 1946 photograph was taken. By the time the contemporary photograph was made, the rifleman's location had been home to the original Las Casuelas Mexican restaurant for many years. Next door, the Canyon Café was in a building with an exterior little changed over the next six decades. (58-083; 59-083.)

The Palm Springs Fire Department at 377 North Palm Canyon Drive was transformed from a volunteer service to a professionally staffed department after the 1938 incorporation of the city of Palm Springs. An adjacent space housed the Palm Springs Police Department at 381 North Palm Canyon Drive when this 1946 photograph was made. As the contemporary photograph shows, the location now provides an outdoor tree-covered dining area for the Azul and Alibi restaurant and bar. (58-032; 58-033.)

This building was subdivided to accommodate a music store at 380 North Palm Canyon Drive, a bowling alley at 378 North Palm Canyon Drive, and a barbershop at 376 North Palm Canyon Drive. A sign at the entrance advertised "open bowling," while a barber awaited a customer when this 1946 photograph was made. A new shop now occupies the building in this 2011 photograph. (59-084; 58-084.)

The Texaco Service Station occupied 399 North Palm Canyon Drive when this 1946 photograph was taken. Except for the Buick on the left, the rest of the cars seem war weary from lack of attention. With the lifting of rationing following the end of World War II, most were anxious to restart lives put on hold for the duration. The contemporary photograph features the Terrace Eateries food court with seven kitchens. It opened in 2006 and closed in 2008. (59-033; 58-033.)

400 North Palm Canyon Drive

An open field in the 400 block of North Palm Canyon Drive provides an unobstructed side view of Our Lady of Solitude Church in 1946. This Class One Historic Site at 151 West Alejo Road was designed by Albert Martin, architect of Los Angeles City Hall. He was selected to design the Spanish Revival church on land acquired from the Southern Pacific Railroad. President Kennedy attended mass here when visiting the Palm Springs area. (28-308.)

Parked on North Palm Canyon Drive, a 1946 Ford convertible awaited its driver. Three separate buildings housed Acme Electrical at 415, Dr. Lynn's office at 419, and the Williams' real estate office at 423. The Williams family no longer uses the office at 423, but business is still active in Palm Springs real estate. A popular restaurant, Hamburger Mary's Bar and Grill, now has the combined 415 and 419 buildings. Desert Legal Aid occupies 423 North Palm Canyon Drive. (58-036; 59-036.)

Monte Vista Apartments at 414 North Palm Canyon Drive was purchased by John and Freda Miller in 1921. With their two sons, Frank and John, they ran the hotel for the next 65 years. In 2005, an Orange County coastal developer purchased the 400 block to build a two-to-four-story building with 100 units and 21,000 square feet of retail space. The contemporary photograph shows the 400 block of North Palm Canyon Drive and North Indian Canyon Drive cleared for the Port Lawrence development. (59-091; 58-091.)

Limelight News, under variant names from the mid-1930s through the mid-1950s, published an alternative to the *Desert Sun* newspaper in Palm Springs. In 1946, it was located at 425 North Palm Canyon Drive. Past issues of *Limelight News* remain an important source for documenting exclusive social events and the activities of visiting celebrities. The location is now a parking lot. (59-038; 58-038.)

Monte Vista Apartments stretched from North Palm Canyon Drive across to North Indian Canyon Drive. Shown in this 1946 photograph is the real estate office of Frank W. Miller at 428 North Palm Canyon Drive. The contemporary photograph shows land for the proposed Port Lawrence project. The land was acquired in two parcels, including one piece from the owner of the Monte Vista Apartments. Upscale shops, galleries, and restaurants were envisioned to be ready as early as 2008. (58-093; 59-093.)

A real estate company and chiropractor occupied half of the building located at 431–439 North Palm Canyon Drive in 1946. The building design likely was influenced by Hollywood. Its occupants served movie stars and producers having Palm Springs retreats just inside their contractually limited driving distance from the studios in Los Angeles (no more than one day away). Units are combined in the contemporary photograph, but the business occupying the space vacated before the 2009 photograph was made. (58-039; 59-039.)

400 NORTH PALM CANYON DRIVE

The Bella Vista Hotel, Lewbel Jewelry, and Muriel Fulton real estate occupied the Mission Revival building at 478–482 North Palm Canyon Drive when this 1946 photograph was taken. The demolition required to clear the land for the Port Lawrence project displaced several businesses, including Edgardo's Café Veracruz, Sublime, House of Kojima, and M Gallery. In 2011, while the block awaits a new destiny, the space sometimes serves as a parking lot for nearby cultural events. (59-095; 58-096.)

A medical doctor, real estate office, and beauty salon occupied 431–439 North Palm Canyon Drive in 1946. There is a section of Palm Springs called the "Movie Colony." There, and in nearby neighborhoods, can be found seasonal homes once occupied by Frank Sinatra and Dinah Shore, among scores of other stars. Especially following World War II, many businesses were established in support of those from the motion picture industry who built homes in Palm Springs. (59-040; 58-040.)

The 1946 photograph shows second-floor rooms of the Bella Vista Hotel overlooking the service garage at 496 North Palm Canyon Drive. After nearly four years of war, attention shifted to a desire for Oldsmobile's "Hydra-Matic" or the stylish Mercury station wagon with a body "made of beautifully grained hard woods." With the train station nine miles from Palm Springs and the closest big city miles beyond that, the car had become a necessity long before the war. (58-096; 59-096.)

When built in the 1920s, this Class One Historic Site at 483 North Palm Canyon Drive was the northernmost residence in Palm Springs. The Spanish Eclectic home was converted to medical offices in the early 1930s. The contemporary photograph features the law offices currently occupying the location. Little has changed in the external features of the building over its more than eight decades on what was Main Street when it was constructed. (58-043; 59-043.)

400 NORTH PALM CANYON DRIVE

The northern gateway to Palm Springs is North Palm Canyon Drive at Alejo Road. Philip Boyd, the first mayor of Palm Springs (1938–1942), was realistic when he considered his neighbors: homeowners prefer keeping the village as they knew it when they came, while business people favor development and expansion. As neighbors, villagers were accountable, sometimes formally and sometimes otherwise, for husbanding the funding needed for public projects. (59-098; 58-098.)

DISCOVER THOUSANDS OF LOCAL HISTORY BOOKS FEATURING MILLIONS OF VINTAGE IMAGES

Arcadia Publishing, the leading local history publisher in the United States, is committed to making history accessible and meaningful through publishing books that celebrate and preserve the heritage of America's people and places.

Find more books like this at
www.arcadiapublishing.com

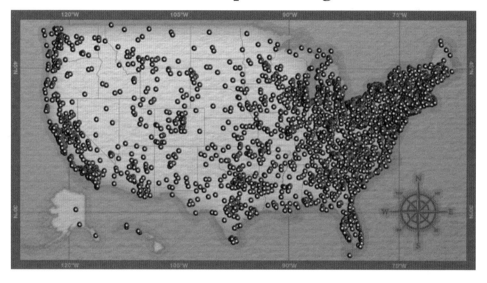

Search for your hometown history, your old stomping grounds, and even your favorite sports team.